A MANUAL FOR THE TRAINING OF SEQUENTIAL MEMORY AND ATTENTION

Pnina S. Klein, EdD

Reading/Learning Disabilities
Adelphi University
Garden City, New York

Allen A. Schwartz, PhD

Educational Clinic
Queens College
of the
City University of New York

ACADEMIC THERAPY PUBLICATIONS
SAN RAFAEL, CALIFORNIA

This book was set in IBM
Century 10 point medium, italic,
and bold type. The display face
was 18 point Bodoni bold.
The paper used was 60 pound White Book
for the text; 65 pound Tuscan Antique for the cover.

Printed in the United States of America.

Table of Contents

INTRODUCTION

    The Training Program   5
    Background.   7
    Research on the Effects of Training
        Sequential Memory and Attention   9

  References. 17

THE TRAINING LESSONS

    Auditory Sequential Memory 27
    Visual Sequential Memory. 61
    Attention 89

  List of Materials 110

Introduction

The Training Program

The Klein-Schwartz program for training sequential memory and attention comprises a complete educational package, appropriate for grades one through three, containing a teacher's manual, suggested worksheets and instructional materials. The teacher's manual provides both the behavioral objectives for each exercise and detailed directions for conducting each lesson. The program provides a comprehensive and self-contained learning module which is intended for use either as a *supplement to the existing classroom reading curriculum* or as a tool for *individualized remediation*.

It is important to note that the materials contained within this manual are presented in a format which simultaneously allows for (1) the training of various components of sequential memory and attention, and (2) the diagnosis of strengths and weaknesses in the sequential memory and attention abilities of each child. The notion of diagnostic teaching in relation to the abilities of memory and attention is of prime importance. What appears to be the same deficit in memory may stem from a variety of causes. A child may experience difficulty in remembering sequences presented auditorily or visually, sequences requiring the processing of information from more than one sensory channel, sequences involving different intervals of delay between presentation and recall, or sequences involving materials of various levels of interest. The possibility that the underlying causes of apparently similar problems in children may differ emphasizes the importance of evaluating the sources of each child's problem on an individual basis (see Tables 1, 2 and 3, pages 24, 58 and 86).

The evaluation aspect is embedded in the training itself. The teacher can follow the sequence of lesson plans and note the child's achievement on each lesson. Since the lessons are coded for the different abilities called for, they enable the evaluation of strengths and weaknesses in specific aspects of memory and attention.

In order to plan a good learning program for a child, it is important to establish what type of information (i.e., visual, auditory, tactile) presented at what particular speed or in what manner enables him to remember or attend better. If a child is found to function well on some of the activities and poorly on others, it is essential to look for a common denominator, a common factor which might be the underlying cause for the difficulty. If such a cause is found in terms of the codes used in the manual, the authors suggest that an educational program be developed which encompasses the following two components: (1) the systematic training in areas of weakness through the use of those lessons focusing on the specific disability, and (2) the strengthening of compensatory abilities which will permit the child to immediately progress in learning, thereby improving self-esteem and confidence.

Each memory lesson plan in the program represents a model lesson which may be used as a basis for developing a variety of additional tasks. In each lesson, the level of task difficulty may be easily manipulated by the trainer, without changing the nature of the task, in any one of the the following ways: (1) by increasing the number of elements in the sequence to be remembered; (2) by varying the amount of time between presentation and recall of the material to be remembered; (3) by requiring the reversal of the sequence both with and without the use of supporting aids; (4) by requiring an intervening activity between presentation and recall.

The lessons are intended for use with a group of seven or eight children working with an adult trainer. They may also be adapted for use in individual remediation or for activities involving the entire class. Naturally, when more than eight children are working together in a group, the usefulness of the program for individual diagnostic teaching is reduced.

The program calls for continuous trainer-student interaction. However, no special training is required of the trainer to conduct the program. It may be easily understood and applied by teachers, teacher aids, paraprofessional and resource persons, as well as parents. Structured into half-hour sessions, the program builds within each lesson and from one lesson to the next. Several of the lessons include explanatory notes clarifying for the trainer various theoretical or procedural aspects of the lesson.

Children like to learn when learning means doing what they like to do. Our training for sequential memory and attention utilizes activities and games that are often viewed as "fun" rather than school-type activities. Teachers will note the usefulness of well-known children games for the purpose of training memory or attention.

Children are often fascinated by the new and different. Thus, the program has attempted to incorporate many novel materials and activities. For example, various lessons involve paper folding, sign language, dramatization, dance and gesture, and musical activity.

In order to enable the teacher to shift from the training of sequential memory to the training of attention using the same materials, pairs of consecutively presented lessons utilize the same materials for training sequential memory in one session and attention in the other. This special arrangement will make it easier for the teacher to reach meaningful conclusions in diagnostic teaching. More specifically, since the same type of materials are used for both memory and attention, a child doing poorly on the memory tasks and doing well on the attention tasks will probably be a child who has no attention problems but does have sequential memory problems.

In summary, the Klein-Schwartz training program presents a systematic approach to the training of auditory and visual sequential memory and attention. It provides a needed additional dimension to available intervention programs for children with reading problems and general learning disability by focusing on the improvement of a mechanism central to the learning process.

Background

A variety of remedial methods have been attempted with learning-disabled children over the last twenty years. Each approach stemmed from a belief in the central importance of a different cognitive or behavioral function in the learning process. For example, Barbara Bateman (1965) has emphasized linguistic remediation, Carl Delacato (1963) has stressed neurological repatterning, Newell Kephart (1960) has suggested a motoric approach, Ray Barsch (1965) based remediation on movement training, and Marianne Frostig (1964) focused on visual-perceptual remediation.

Recently, however, the role of sequential memory in reading has been demonstrated in research, revealing disturbances of memory in children with learning disorders (Heriot, 1973; Hirshorn, 1969; Rugel, 1974). Auditory sequential memory (ASM) was found to differentiate significantly between retarded and normal children (Gallagher and Lucito, 1961; Kirk, 1968) as well as between poor and normal readers (Bannatyne, 1971, 1974; Rugel, 1974). The use of ASM for predicting success in reading has also been suggested (Chall et al., 1963; and Hirshorn, 1969).

The training of auditory skills in the remediation of reading problems has been suggested before (Deutsch, 1964; Durrell and Murphy, 1963; Weiner, 1966; Wepman, 1960). However, none of these available programs attempted to train and evaluate isolated abilities within the sequential memory and attention domain.

Sequential Memory

The commanding influence of memory on learning is accounted for in various behavior models (McDonald, 1965; Wepman, 1960; Bateman, 1965). Memory is generally considered to encompass both long-term memory and short-term or immediate memory. Immediate memory is most involved in those mental activities which are dependent upon rote learning. In order to reproduce rhythm patterns, or sequences of digits, words, or sentences, one must rely heavily on sequential memory (Myers & Hammill, 1969).

It has been suggested that children with reading difficulty have problems in transferring information from one sensory modality to another (Birch & Belmont, 1964). These investigators have reported that poor readers have difficulty repeating a sequence even within the same modality. These findings suggest that the difficulties experienced by poor readers in cross-modal transfer could be explained by poor sequential memory.

Hirshorn (1969) tested auditory skills in kindergarten children and assessed reading achievement at the end of second grade. He found that the auditory sequential memory subtest on the *Illinois Test of Psycholinguistic Abilities* (ITPA) was correlated with the reading tests on the *California Achievement Test*. He concluded that ASM was useful in predicting success in reading. Jean Chall et al. (1963) reported that sound blending ability (which requires sequential memory) in the first grade was correlated significantly with third grade silent reading.

Studies comparing scores of different populations on the ITPA (Kirk, 1966) suggest that retarded and minimally brain-damaged children demonstrate poor functioning on that part of the test measuring automatic sequential abilities rather than the part measuring higher conceptual abilities.

Attention

Problems of attention are variously labeled as distractibility, hyperactivity, hyperawareness, hyperirritability, or short attention span. All of these concepts refer to the inability to screen out superfluous, extraneous stimuli. Although distractibility and hyperactivity are often noted in the behavior of children with brain dysfunction (Cruickshank et al., 1961; McCarthy & McCarthy, 1969; Strauss & Kephart, 1955), Schulman, Kaspar, and Throne (1965) concluded that "since the same symptoms may appear with dysfunctions other than brain damage, the diagnosis of brain damage should be used sparingly." John Hagen (1967) suggested that the ability to attend develops with age. He found in children of grades 1, 3, 5, and 7 a clear development of the ability to attend to relevant stimulus features in the presence of distractors.

William Rohwer (1970) following a review of the research on attention states that the question of how attention may be elicited in children and maintained or controlled thereafter is largely unanswered.

Existing research data suggest that attention can be trained. Both extrinsic and intrinsic reinforcement were found effective in controlling attention through verbal approval (Fish and McNamara, 1963) and through properties of the visual stimuli attended to (Berlyne, 1958; Fantz, 1961; and Hershenson, 1967).

In Piaget's theory of cognitive development, unstable attention and distractibility are characteristics of the sensory-motor stage of cognitive development, whereas more advanced stages are characterized by more attentional control.

In summary, although the significance of attention in the learning situation has been recognized, the systematic training of attention in the schools has been largely neglected.

Research on the Effects of Training
Sequential Memory and Attention

As previously indicated, sequential memory and attention are demonstrated indicators of early reading readiness and success; deficits in these two abilities have been linked consistently with both reading failure and general learning disability. Most significant is the fact that research recently completed (Klein and Schwartz, 1976) indicates the "trainability" of both auditory sequential memory and attention, and the carry-over of gains in sequential memory into the area of reading.

The goal of this research was to examine the possible causal relationship between ASM and reading by focusing on the following questions: (1) Can auditory sequential memory in young children be improved through training?

(2) What are the effects of such training on the reading ability of thildren with reading problems?

Subjects

The subjects were 33 girls and 59 boys, with a mean age of 8-2, attending second and third grade in four schools in Queens, New York. All subjects were of average intelligence, were reading at least one grade below grade level (mean reading accuracy deficit = 2.1 grades), and were significantly below average on two measures of *Auditory Sequential Memory* (ASM).

Procedure

The research design included (a) pretesting, (b) training, and (c) posttesting. Children identified by their teachers as being behind grade level in reading were pretested individually in reading accuracy and comprehension, auditory sequential memory, auditory discrimination, attention, arithmetic, and verbal intelligence. Out of 189 subjects tested, 92 scored below average on measures of both reading and ASM.

The 92 subjects were then randomly assigned to either an experimental group receiving ASM training, or to one of three control groups providing either attention training, cognitive enrichment, or no intervention. The training of subjects was accomplished in 25 half-hour training sessions conducted three times per week in the schools. At the completion of the intervention, all subjects were evaluated on the measures used for the pre-training testing.

Findings

Auditory sequential memory and reading were found to improve in all the subject groups; however, the group receiving ASM training showed a significantly larger gain on the ASM measures and on reading accuracy (See Figure 1). Specifically, the ASM group showed twice the gain in ASM (43 percent), visual sequential memory (18 percent), and reading accuracy (95 percent) as compared to the other training and control groups. Furthermore, the obtained gain in ASM was significantly greater for the second graders as compared to the third graders. The training of attention as well as the training of ASM was found to have a facilitative effect on auditory discrimination ability.

Based on the findings, it may be conclude that ASM can be improved through training and that this improvement does have a facilitative effect on reading accuracy. Hence, a causal relationship between these two abilities has been demonstrated. The findings demonstrate the transferability of observed gains from the auditory to the visual modality, and suggest the existence of a critical period for the development of ASM. This study lends support for the important role played by ASM as a cognitive ability basic to reading, and suggests the need for an additional dimension in the intervention programs available for children with reading disabilities.

No available program to date has attempted to provide systematic and extensive materials for the training and evaluation of the memory and attention component exclusively. An educational package which provides for the programmatic improvement of sequential memory and attention through training would constitute an important asset to all those concerned with teaching children to read.

Figure 1

WISC—R DIGIT SPAN—TOTAL

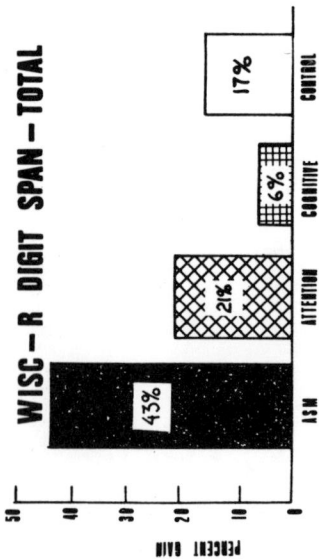

ASM 45%
ATTENTION 21%
COGNITIVE 6%
CONTROL 17%

WISC—R DIGIT SPAN—FORWARD

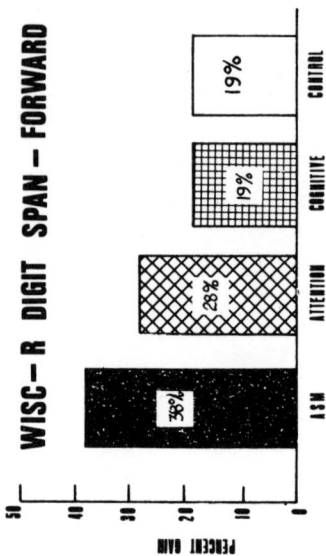

ASM 38%
ATTENTION 28%
COGNITIVE 19%
CONTROL 19%

WISC—R DIGIT SPAN—BACKWARD

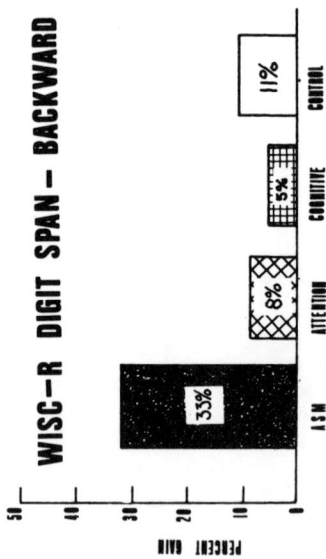

ASM 33%
ATTENTION 8%
COGNITIVE 5%
CONTROL 11%

ITPA AUDITORY SEQUENTIAL MEMORY

ASM 15%
ATTENTION 6%
COGNITIVE 6%
CONTROL 2%

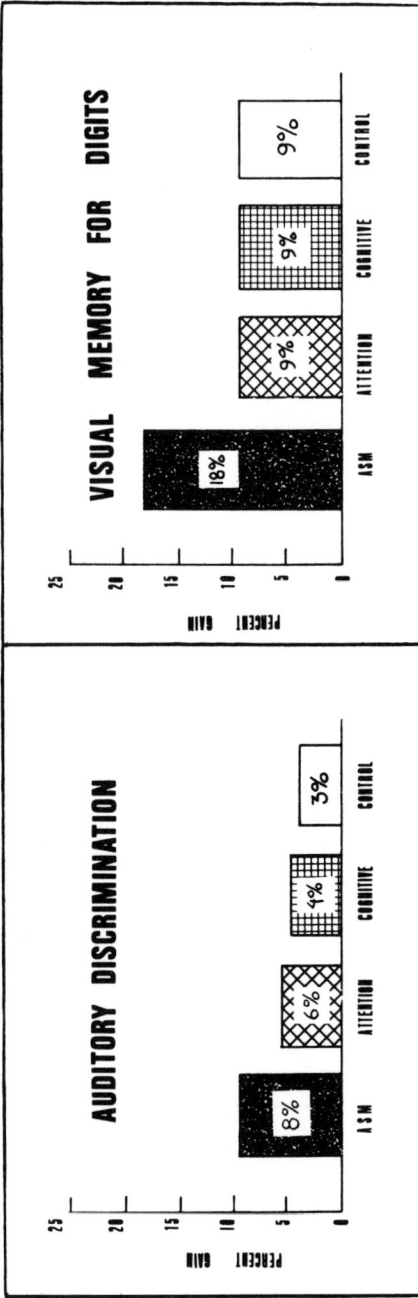

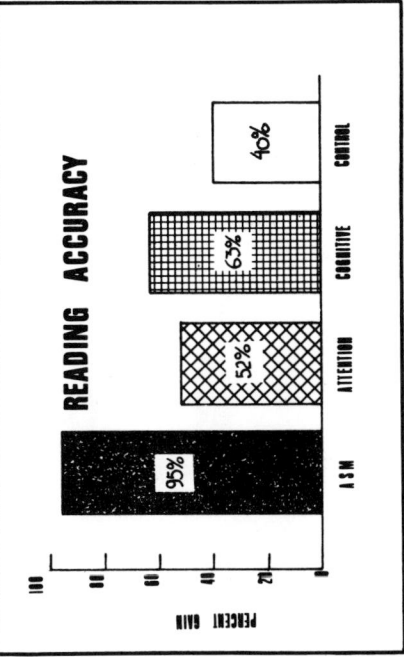

Figure 1

Percent gain in Auditory and Visual Sequential Memory, Auditory Discrimination, and Reading Accuracy following each of the four interventions.

REFERENCES

Bannatyne, Alex. *Language, reading, and learning disabilities*. Springfield: Charles C Thomas, 1971.

Bannatyne, Alex. Programs, materials, and techniques. *Journal of Learning Disabilities*, 1974, 7, 272-277.

Barsch, Raymond H. *Movigenic curriculum*. Madison, Wisconsin: Bureau for Handicapped Children, 1965.

Bateman, Barbara D. An educator's view of a diagnostic approach to learning disorders. In Jerome Hellmuth (Ed.), *Learning disorders, Vol. I*. Seattle, Washington: Special Child Publications, 1965.

Berlyne, D. E. The influence of complexity and novelty in visual figures on orienting responses. *Journal of Experimental Psychology*, 1958, 55, 289-296.

Birch, Herbert G., and Belmont, L. Auditory-visual interaction in normal and retarded readers. *American Journal of Orthopsychiatry*, 1964, 34, 852-861.

Chall, J. Roswell, F., and Blumenthal, S. H. Auditory blending ability: a factor in success in beginning reading. *Reading Teacher*, 1963, 17, 113-118.

Cruickshank, William M. A teaching method for brain-injured and hyperactive children: a demonstration-pilot study. Syracuse, New York: Syracuse University Press, 1961. (Special Education and Rehabilitation Monograph Series No. 6.)

Delacato, Carl H. *The diagnosis and treatment of speech and reading problems*. Springfield, Illinois: Charles C Thomas, 1963.

Deutsch, Cynthia P. Auditory discrimination and learning social factors. *Merrill-Palmer Quarterly*, 1964, 10, 277-296.

Durrel, Donald, and Murphy, H. The auditory discrimination factor in reading readiness and reading disability. *Education*, 1963, 73, 556-560.

Fantz, R. L. The origin of form perception. *Scientific American*, 1961, 204, 66-72.

Fisch, R. I., and McNamara, H. J. Conditioning of attention as a factor in perceptual learning. *Perceptual and Motor Skills*, 1963, 17, 891-907.

Frostig, Marianne, and Horne, David. *The Frostig Program for the development of visual perception*. Chicago, Illinois: Follet Publishing Co., 1964.

Gallagher, James J., and Lucito, L. Intellectual patterns of gifted, average, and retarded. *Exceptional Children*, 1961, 27, 479-482.

Hagen, John W. The effect of distraction on selective attention. *Child Development*, 1967, 38, 684-694.

Heriot, James T. Memory/attention versus visual/perceptual correlates of learning disorders in a pediatric population. Paper presented at the Annual Meeting of the Society for Pediatric Research, San Francisco, 1973.

Hershenson, M. Development of the perception of form. *Psychological Bulletin,* 1967, 67, 326-336.

Hirshorn, A. A comparison of the predictive validity of the revised Stanford-Binet Intelligence Scale and Illinois Test of Psycholinguistic Abilities. *Exceptional Children,* 1969, 35, 517-521.

Kephart, Newell C. *The slow learner in the classroom.* Columbus, Ohio: Charles E. Merrill Books, Inc., 1960.

Kirk, Samuel A. *Diagnosis and remediation of psycholinguistic abilities.* Urbana, Illinois: University of Illinois Press, 1966.

Kirk, Samuel A. Illinois Test of Psycholinguistic Abilities: Its origin and implications. In Jerome Hellmuth (Ed.), *Learning disorders, Vol. III.* Seattle Washington: Special Child Publications, 1968.

McCarthy, James J., and McCarthy, Joan F. *Learning disabilities.* Boston: Allyn and Bacon, Inc., 1969.

McDonald, F. J. *Symbolic model of the learner in educational psychology.* Belmont, California: Wadsworth, 1965.

Myers, Patricia I., and Hammill, Donald D. *Methods for learning disorders.* New York, New York: John Wiley, 1969.

Rohwer, William D. Implications of cognitive development for education. In P. H. Mussen (Ed.), *Carmichael's manual of child psychology (3rd ed.),* Vol. I, 1970, 1379-1454.

Rugel, Robert P. WISC subtest scores of disabled readers: a review with respect to Bannatyne's recategorization. *Journal of Learning Disabilities,* 1974, 7, 57-16.

Strauss, A. A., and Kephart, N. C. *Psychopathology and education of the brain-injured child: progress in theory and clinic,* Vol. II. New York, New York: Grune and Stratton, 1955.

Shulman, Jerome L., Kaspar, Joseph C., and Throne, Francis M. *Brain damage and behavior.* Springfield, Illinois: Charles C Thomas, 1965.

Weiner, J. Motivation and memory. *Psychological Monograph,* 1966, 80 (No. 626).

Wepman, Joseph M. Auditory discrimination, speech, and reading. *Elementary School,* 1960, 60, 325-333.

Training Manual
for
Sequential Memory and Attention

Lessons
in
Auditory Sequential Memory

Table 1

Table 1

Summary Table of the Sensory Channels of Input and Output
for All Auditory Sequential Memory Lesson Plans

Lesson Number	Input				Output			
	Auditory	Visual	Motor	Tactile	Auditory or Verbal	Visual	Motor	Tactile
1	x	x			x		x	
2	x				x		x	
3	x	x			x			
4	x				x		x	
5	x					x	x	
6	x				x		x	
7	x	x			x			
8	x					x	x	

9		x		x				x
10		x		x				x
11					x			x
12		x	x		x			x
13				x				x
14				x				x
15				x				x
16				x				x
17				x			x	x
18				x				x
19		x						x
20		x					x	x

INTRODUCTORY LESSON

THE MEANING OF SEQUENCE

Objective: The student will be able to explain what is meant by a "sequence" and give examples of sequences.

Materials: None.

Procedure: Say, "Today we will learn the meaning of a new word—*sequence*. Things in a sequence are things that come one after the other in a certain order. If you change the order, then you have changed the sequence. For example, the days of the week make a sequence; Monday always comes after Sunday, and Tuesday always comes after Monday, and so on. Let's all repeat the sequence of the days of the week out loud. (Recite days of the week aloud together.) What other sequences of things can you think of? Remember, a sequence is a group of things that come one after the other according to a certain order."

Examples of sequences which may be suggested include seasons of the year, numbers, letters of the alphabet, meals of the day, time periods of the day (morning, noon, afternoon, evening), ages and grades, and sequential activities (certain sports, cooking, dance steps, etc.). Have the students discuss the sequential aspects of these examples; encourage them to act out sequential activities.

AUDITORY SEQUENTIAL MEMORY (ASM)

LESSON 1

Objective: The student will identify and correct errors made in the auditory presentation of his telephone number.

The student will position himself in a sequence according to some predesignated criterion.

Materials: None.

Procedure: Introduce the importance of keeping the items of a sequence in the correct order through the example of telephone numbers. Have a student give you his telephone number. Repeat it to him, changing a number one time, reversing two numbers another time, and so on. Have the student identify and correct the errors made in his telephone number. Give each student a chance at this activity.

Next, demonstrate the different sequences which may be formed using the students themselves. Say, "I want you all to write your last names on the chalkboard." After this is done, say, "now let's all form a line according to the alphabetical sequence of our last names." Demonstrate to the students how this is done. Repeat the procedure, with the students forming lines based upon the following sequences:

(a) alphabetical order of last name
(b) alphabetical order of first name
(c) birthday
(d) age
(e) height

Encourage the students to suggest additional criteria which may be used to sequence the class.

ASM

LESSON 2

Objective: The students will play a melodic sequence after they have heard it once.

Materials: Melody Bells and musical notes.

Procedure: Place the Melody Bells in front of the students and allow each student to "try out" the different bells and listen to their sound. Say, "Now, I am going to play three notes of a song. Close your eyes and listen carefully. When I am through, I want one of you to try to repeat the same melody on the Melody Bells right after me. You may try out several bells before you choose the correct ones." When one student has identified the three notes through trial and error and has repeated the sequence, allow other students to follow the procedure.

Repeat the procedure by adding additional notes to build longer sequences within the same melody (different melodies may be used).

The trainer should allow the students the opportunity to enjoy recognizing the melodies which are being constructed in the process of adding notes. An appreciation for the role of sequence in music should be encouraged.

ASM

LESSON 3

Objective: The student will remember a sequence of objects in correct order and repeat it verbally.

Materials: Black and white drawings of common objects.

Procedure: Each student in turn is presented with a set of ten pictured objects. Say, "I am going to name some of the pictures in front of you. Point to each one as I say it. After I finish, you say them without looking at the pictures. Try to say them in the same order as you pointed to them."

Start with sequence of three pictures for each child. After each child has succeeded, increase the number of items by one and repeat procedure.

Note: Students' motivation to improve their sequential memory may be enhanced by means of two general methods: (1) Providing a reward that is intrinsic to the nature of the task, i.e., telling each child how many things in a sequence he remembered correctly each session, and (2) Providing a reward that is based on achievement but is extrinsic to the nature of the task, i.e., handing out stars or other small prizes to children who improve their sequential memory from lesson to lesson or within one lesson.

ASM

LESSON 4

Objective: The student will follow a series of verbally presented directions and repeat the directions verbally in the correct sequence.

Materials: None.

Procedure: Say, "I am going to tell you some things that I want you to do. Listen carefully and then try to follow the directions in the order I said them. After you finish, I want you to tell me the things you did in the same order that you did them."

Begin by demonstrating the procedure to the students with a series of three directions (e.g., write name on chalkboard, open door, sit on chair). Then repeat this procedure with each student, starting with a series of three directions. After each child has succeeded, increase difficulty by making the series longer.

Sample Directions:

1. Write name on chalkboard.
2. Open door, close door.
3. Sit on chair.
4. Hop or skip, forward or backward.
5. Open book, close book.
6. Draw circle, square, triangle on paper.
7. Touch toes, head, knees.
8. Lift chair.
9. Clap, snap fingers.
10. Sharpen pencil.
11. Erase chalkboard.

Input: Auditory
Output: Visual/Motor

ASM

LESSON 5

Objective: The student will string beads in a correct color and/or shape sequence following verbal instructions, and will repeat the sequence verbally.

Materials: Box of differently colored and shaped beads and bead string.

Procedure: Place a box of beads (different colors and shapes) in front of the student. Say, "I am going to tell you which beads to string and in what order. Listen carefully and when I am finished, I want you to repeat immediately what I said and then string your beads exactly as I told you." When the student has completed the task, ask the student to repeat verbally his sequence of beads without looking at it.

Start with a sequence of three colors only for each child. After each child has succeeded, increase the sequence by one color and repeat procedure.

The task can be made more difficult by introducing various combinations of colors and shapes into the sequence (e.g., red square, blue triangle, green circle, etc.) or by adding different multiples of each bead to be strung (e.g., two red squares, three blue circles, one yellow triangle, etc.).

ASM

LESSON 6

Objective: The student will step from color to color according to a verbally presented sequence, and repeat the sequence verbally. The student will repeat a list of colors presented verbally.

Materials: Eight color cards.

Procedure: Arrange the eight color cards on the floor in random fashion. Say, "I am going to tell each of you what colors to step on. Listen carefully and when I am through, you step on the colors in the order that I said them." When the student has done this, ask him to repeat the sequence of colors verbally. Begin with three colors. After each child has successfully completed this task, give each child another set of three colors and ask him to repeat it verbally (without stepping on the colors this time).

To increase the difficulty of the task, repeat procedure with four colors. For interest, the students may be asked to hop or jump from one color to the next.

Input: Auditory/Visual
Output: Verbal

ASM

LESSON 7

Objective: The student will remember a series of land-marks in correct sequence, and will recall the sequence forward and backward.

Materials: Set of landmark cards.

Procedure: Each student in turn is presented with three cards, each depicting an object that serves as a landmark. Say, "I want you to make believe that on the way to school, you have to pass each of the things pictured on your cards." Point to each card as its name is mentioned. "Now, I want you to try to remember each of the things that you pass on the way to school, in the order that you would pass them, without looking at your cards." After the student has repeated the sequence verbally repeat the procedure, but this time ask the student to make believe he is going from school to home, thereby *reversing* the sequence.

Begin with a sequence of three landmarks for each child. After each child has succeeded, increase the number of landmarks by one and repeat the procedure.

SAMPLE LANDMARKS

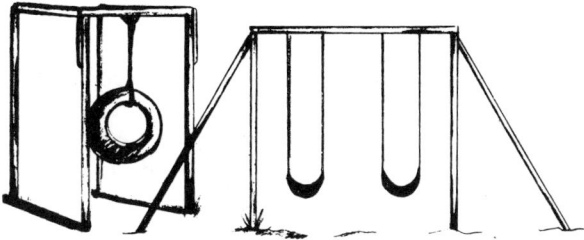

ASM

LESSON 8

Objective: The student will remember a series of numbers and/or letters in a correct sequence and connect them on a worksheet.

Materials: Worksheet with random numbers and letters.

Procedure: The students use a worksheet on which numbers and letters are printed in random fashion. Say, "I am going to say a list of letters. Listen carefully and when I am finished, I want each of you to draw a line connecting the letters I said in the same order I said them. After we are finished connecting the letters, we will say them aloud in the same order that we connected them."

Start with a sequence of three letters and increase by one for each trial.

The same procedure can be repeated with numbers only. The task can be made more difficult by introducing mixed sequences of letters and numbers. Start by including only one number in a sequence of letters.

ASM

LESSON 9

Objective: The student will duplicate a sequence of hand clapping with and without the aid of visual cues.

Materials: None.

Procedure: Say, "I am going to clap my hands in a special way. I want you to listen carefully and when I am finished I will ask one of you (or all of you) to clap your hands in the same way."

Begin by clapping where hands may be seen by students. After each student has succeeded at this task several times, say, "Now I am going to clap my hands under the table so you can only hear the clapping but you cannot see it. Listen carefully, and when I finish, try to clap your hands to make the same sounds that I made." Repeat sequences in this manner without the aid of visual cues.

The task becomes more challenging as the sequences become longer and more complex.

1. C ... C ... C
2. CC ... CC ... CC
3. C ... CC ... C ... CC
4. C ... C ... CC ... C
5. CCC ... CC ... C

Input: Auditory
Output: Verbal/Motor

ASM

LESSON 10

Objective: The student will step from number to number (or letter to letter) according to a verbally presented sequence and repeat the sequence verbally, both forward and backward.

Materials: Number and letter cards.

Procedure: Arrange the number and letter cards on the floor in random fashion. Say, "I am going to tell each of you what letters to step on. Listen carefully and when I finish, you step on the letters in the same order as I said them to you." When the student has completed this part, ask him to repeat the sequence of letters verbally, first forward (in the order he stepped on them) and then *backward*. If a student has difficulty in reversing the sequence, have him write the series of letters on the chalkboard in the forward order and then read them off the board in the reversed order. Gradually, eliminate the student's dependence on the written sequence by having him repeat the reversed sequence without looking at the board.

Begin with a sequence of three letters, and increase the sequence by one unit after each child has succeeded. Gradually introduce numbers into the sequence to make the task more difficult.

Note: The materials used in this exercise may be adapted for the purpose of spelling actual words through a given sequence of letters which are stepped out. The importance of letter *sequence* may be emphasized in this way, by demonstrating the different words which may be spelled out using the same three or four letters in various sequences. "Sounding out" may be combined with the stepping exercise to underscore the sequential aspect of the sounding out process.

Input: Auditory or Tactile
Output: Motor or Verbal

ASM

LESSON 11

Objective: The student will repeat from memory a sequence of letters whispered to him or "written" on his back.

Materials: None.

Procedure: For this activity students should be seated in pairs. Ask one student to come up to you. Say, "I am going to whisper several letters to you. Try to remember them because I want you to write them one after the other on your partner's back. Write them out with the eraser end of your pencil. After you have finished writing all of the letters, have your partner say them out loud in the same order you wrote them." Let each in turn carry out the task; the trainer should monitor their performance and correct all errors.

Change the roles of the partners in each pair so that every child will have a chance to try out his memory for a sequence of items "written" on his back. The lesson may be repeated using numbers instead of letters.

Note: This is a task involving auditory input and motor output for the student who is required to "write" the sequence of letters on his partner's back. For the partner, however, the task entails tactile input and verbal output. This task presents a good example of a simple task which requires the processing of different sensory information depending upon the role of each participant.

ASM

LESSON 12

Objective: The student will retrieve hidden geometric shapes, by touch, according to a previously presented verbal sequence.

Materials: Set of geometric shapes in a bag.

Procedure: Show the students the bag with the different geometric shapes and identify each of the shapes by name. Put them back into the bag and say; "I am going to say a sequence of three shapes. Listen carefully, and when I am through I want you to reach into the bag, feel the different shapes, and take out the ones that I said. Once you have the shapes, arrange them in the same order as I said them."

Begin with sequences of three shapes and increase the length of the sequences gradually. For additional complexity the students may be asked to remember sequences composed of multiples of shapes to be selected (i.e., two squares, one triangle, three circles).

ASM

LESSON 13

Objective: The student will repeat from memory a verbally presented list of picnic items:

a. in no particular sequence
b. in a specified sequence

Materials: None.

Procedure: Say, "Let us pretend that we are going out on a picnic and you are asked to make up a list of things to bring from home. Suppose you had written everything down but forgot your note, and you have to remember your list."

Ask every student to say a list of things that he would choose to take with him on a picnic (stop after first four items); then ask him to repeat the list from memory—first in any order he wishes and later with an emphasis on sequence. If the student forgets an item while repeating the items in sequence, say, "What comes after . . .?"

Note: It is commonly believed that sequential memory, since it requires memory of a sequence of items, is more difficult for a child than the recall of items in no particular sequence. This is not always the case. Some children rely on their auditory associations as the principal means of coding information in memory; focusing on sequence might actually make the task easier for these children. For others who rely on verbal labeling and cognitive categorization, recall with no emphasis on sequence may be easier. This session may help the teacher to focus on this aspect of individual differences in the memory strategies of children.

ASM

LESSON 14

Objective: The student will remember a sentence whispered to him and repeat it accurately.

Materials: None.

Procedure: Say, "We are going to play a game called 'telephone'; we are going to see how well a sentence can 'travel' from one student to the other without losing or changing words. I want you to sit in a circle; I am going to whisper a sentence to one of you; the same child has to remember the sentence and whisper it exactly as I said it, to his neighbor. His neighbor has to whisper the sentence to the next neighbor and so on, until all of the students have participated. The student who is last will say the sentence out loud so that everyone can hear if the 'telephone' worked well." Continue this procedure for various sentences differing in length. Start with a different student each time.

Sample Sentences:
1. I like to go to the zoo.
2. I love to feed the monkeys.
3. I like to feed the monkeys at the zoo.
4. Johnny and I always go watch monkeys in the zoo.

ASM

LESSON 15

Objective: The student will remember a series of sounds in order and blend them together into meaningful words.

Materials: None.

Procedure: Say, "I am going to say some sounds; I want you to listen carefully and try to repeat the sounds in the same order I said them, but closer together. If you succeed you will find that the sounds make up a word."

Let each student try to blend the sounds presented to him. When three sounds are blended correctly, proceed to four sounds, etc. *Reverse Procedure:* Ask every student to volunteer a word; then ask the students to break the word up into its sequence of component sounds.

Sample Words:
1. u - p
2. c - ow
3. c - a - t
4. b - i - g
5. st - u - d - ent
6. te - le - vi - sion

ASM

LESSON 16

Objective: The student will recall a verbally presented list of food items following intervening activities.

Materials: None.

Procedure: Say, "We are going to play a make-believe game. Let's make believe that we are in a big new school cafeteria where everyone can get everything he would like to eat. Some of us have to work at this cafeteria too. Some of us will be the customers who come to eat at the cafeteria; others will be the cooks and waiters." Break the students up into groups of three; assign to one of them the role of a "customer"; to a second the role of the "waiter"; and to the third the role of the "cook."

Continue by saying, "If you are a customer you will tell the waiter three things that you would like to eat. The waiter will remember your order and tell it to the cook. The cook will make believe he is preparing the food and will hand it back to the waiter, while repeating the list of ordered foods. The waiter will then bring the food back to the customer and repeat the list of foods as he serves them. Finally, the customer will repeat the list to make sure that he has received all the things that he asked for, in the correct sequence."

In order to increase the complexity of this task, the customer may increase the number of food items which he orders. In addition, the roles played by the three students in each group can be rotated so every student gets a chance to act out every role.

Note: The "cook" is required to repeat the order after engaging in "preparation" of the food. Thus, the role of cook requires short-term sequential memory following some intervening activity. A student's performance in this role as compared to his performance in the other roles may indicate how well he can remember a series of things when he is required to do something between hearing the series and repeating it.

ASM

LESSON 17

Objective: The student will repeat and reverse a sequence of new names.

Materials: None.

Procedure: Say, "We all wonder at times what it would feel like if we had been given a different name. Each of you now has a chance to choose another first name for himself. I am going to ask each of you to tell his 'new' name to the group. I want you to try and remember the new names of everyone in the group in the same order you hear them."

Start with each student in the group repeating three of the new names in sequence; then ask the students to reverse that sequence.

Note: This task requires an association between the new name and the real name of each student, or between the new name and his face. By asking the students *how* they remembered the sequence of new names, the teacher may learn about the student's memory strategies; i.e., do they rely more on verbal associations (real names) or on visual associations (faces)?

ASM

LESSON 18

Objective: The student will remember in order a list of rhymes presented for a target word.

Materials: None.

Procedure: Say, "I am going to say a word, and then a few words that rhyme with it. Listen carefully, and when I am through I want each of you to repeat the word and the words rhyming with it, in the same order as I said them."

Present one of the target words, followed by three of the words that rhyme with it. Let all the students attempt each sequence; be sure to let a different child be first, second, etc., with every new series that is presented. Increase the sequences by one word as the students succeed.

Sample rhyming series:

1. hat, cat, sat, pat, mat, bat, chat, flat
2. hare, care, mare, dare, stare, chair, fair, bear, tear
3. light, might, night, fight, right, tight, height, fright
4. book, look, took, nook, cook, brook, shook, crook
5. car, star, far, jar, scar, bar, mar
6. cake, bake, take, rake, shake, make, flake, break, steak
7. jet, get, met, set, bet, let, fret, pet
8. rose, nose, hose, close, chose, toes, doze, froze, suppose
9. rest, best, nest, chest, pest, crest, test, arrest, jest
10. hit, sit, mitt, bit, spit, slit, knit, fit, kit, lit, pit

ASM

LESSON 19

Objective: The student will first associate dance steps with their names, and then repeat a sequence of steps forward and backward following verbal instructions.

Materials: None.

Procedure: Say, "I am going to teach you the names of five dance steps. Watch me while I demonstrate them to you and see if you can remember their names." Demonstrate the steps for the students (see examples below) and test the students to be sure they have learned the steps and their names.

Next say, "I am going to tell you some steps that I want you to do. Listen carefully and then try to do the steps in the same order I said them. After you have done this, I want you to do the steps in the reverse order, starting with the last step in the sequence and ending with the first." Demonstrate the entire procedure for the students.

Begin with sequences of three steps and increase the number of steps as the students improve their performance. You may wish to introduce additional steps in order to maintain interest or increase difficulty.

Sample steps:

1. Right tap: move the right foot to the right, tap floor, and return to standing position.

   Left tap: move the left foot to the left, tap floor, and return to standing position.

2. Right cross: cross the right leg over the left

leg, tap floor and return to standing position.

Left cross: cross the left leg over the right leg, tap floor, and return to standing position.

3. Forward and backward hop: self-explanatory.

4. Right and left twirl: spin to the right or left on the toes of the feet.

5. Right and left kick: kick leg in "chorus-line" fashion.

Input: Visual and Auditory

Output: Motor

COMBINED LESSON FOR ASM, VSM, AND ATT

LESSON 20

Objective: The student will carry out a sequence of directions that will result in the creation of an oragami (paper folding) object.

Materials: Folding paper.

Procedure: Say, "Today we are going to make things from paper; this art is called 'oragami.' In order to make something from paper, you have to make it one step at a time. If I change the order in which I do the folding, what I am trying to make will not come out right."

Follow directions and create object number one. Then, with another piece of paper, repeat the procedure, but change the order of one folding step, thereby demonstrating to the students that if the step-by-step sequence is not followed correctly, the desired object will not come out right.

"I will give you detailed directions to create something from paper. Listen and observe me carefully. When I am through, you will start working."

The paper folding directions should be presented to the students in sequences of two or three steps at a time until the desired object is created. Read the directions to the students and demonstrate them as you read. Make sure that the students do not follow the paper folding directions one step at a time, but rather carry out sequences of direction following their demonstration by the trainer.

As the students repeat each paper folding exercise, encourage them to remember longer sequences of directions, leading up to the production of the entire object from memory.

SAMPLE PAPER FOLDING EXERCISES

Hat

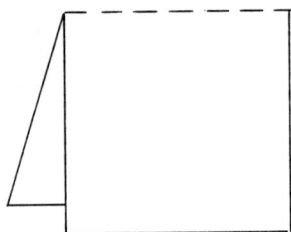

1. **Fold paper in half.**

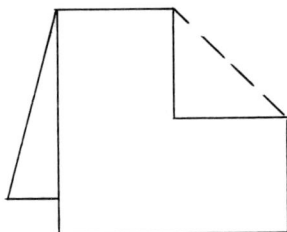

2. **Fold down one corner.**

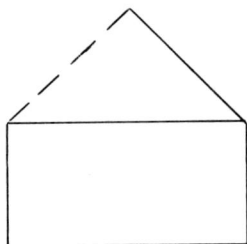

3. **Fold down other corner.**

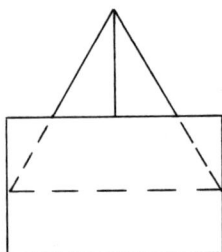

4. **Fold up front flap.**

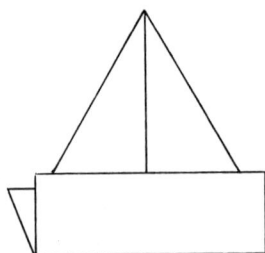

5. **Fold up other flap and open to form hat.**

Basket

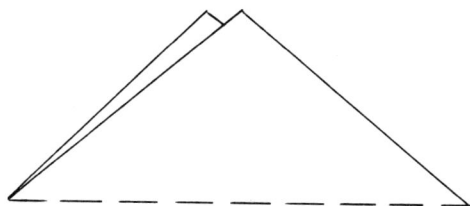

1. Fold paper in half diagonally.

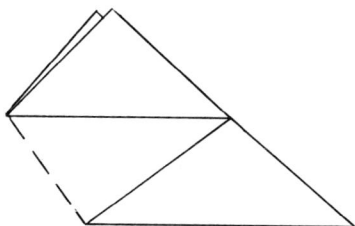

2. Fold one corner to the mid-point of the opposite side.

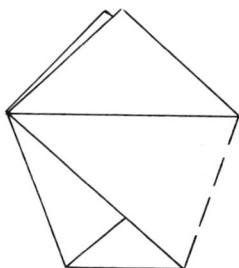

3. Fold other corner in similar manner.

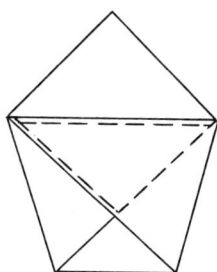

4. Fold down one flap and open to form basket.

"Fortune Telling" Pinwheel

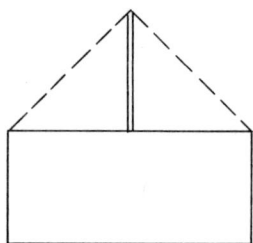

1. Fold two top corners into center.

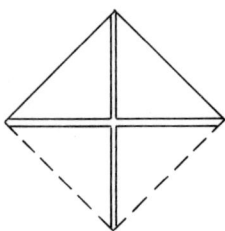

2. Fold two bottom corners into center.

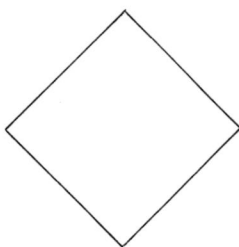

3. Turn over.

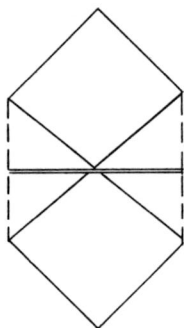

4. Fold two side corners into center.

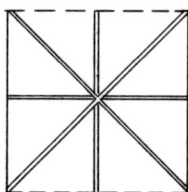

5. Fold top and bottom corners into center.

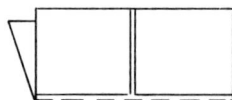

6. Fold in half and crease.

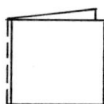

7. Fold in half again and crease.

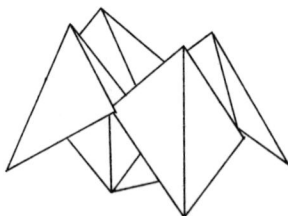

8. Open to position #5 and insert fingers under flaps to form pinwheel.

Lessons
in
Visual Sequential Memory

Table 2

Table 2

Summary Table of the Sensory Channels of Input and Output
for All Visual Sequential Memory Lesson Plans

Lesson Number	Input				Output			
	Auditory	Visual	Motor	Tactile	Auditory or Verbal	Visual	Motor	Tactile
1		x				x	x	
2		x				x	x	
3		x				x	x	
4		x					x	
5		x				x	x	
6		x				x	x	
7		x				x	x	
8		x				x	x	

9	×	×				×	
10	×	×				×	
11	×		×	×		×	
12	×	×		×		×	
13	×	×				×	
14	×	×				×	
15	×	×				×	
16	×	×				×	
17		×				×	
18						×	
19	×					×	
20	×					×	×

VISUAL SEQUENTIAL MEMORY (VSM)

LESSON 1

Objective: The student will remember a designated sequence of visual symbols and reproduce it.

Materials: Two sets of eight visual symbol cards:

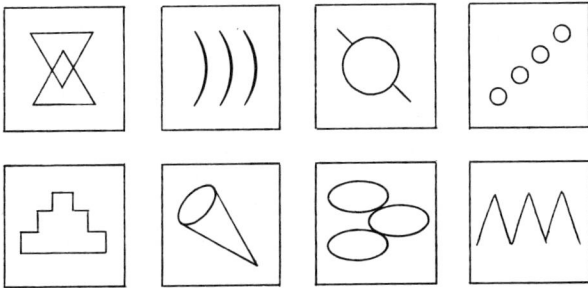

Procedure: Arrange a sequence of two of the visual symbol cards on the ledge of the chalkboard. Have students in the group hold the cards from the second set, with each student holding a different card. Have each student first view the sequence displayed on the board, and then move his classmates around in an attempt to reproduce the identical sequence. Say to one student: "I am going to show you a sequence of cards. Look at them carefully and try to remember the cards and the sequence they are in. When you are ready, turn with your back to the board and try to choose the same cards being held by your classmates. Put your classmates in the same order as the cards were on the board." Correct all mistakes.

Start with sequences of two visual symbols for each student. After each has succeeded, increase the number of items by one and repeat the procedure.

VSM

LESSON 2

Objective: The students will play a melodic sequence after receiving a sequence of visual cues.

Materials: Melody Bells.

Procedure: Place the Melody Bells in front of the students and say: "I am going to make believe that I play part of a song on the Melody Bells, but I will not ring them so that you will not hear any sound. Watch me carefully and try to remember which bells I touch and in what order. When I am through, one of you will come up and try to ring the bells in the same order as I touched them."

Start with a different sequence of three notes for each student. Allow each student to have at least one try, then increase the sequence for students who are successful in carrying out the task.

VSM

LESSON 3

Objective: The student will remember a sequence of pictured objects, and rearrange them into the correct order after shuffling.

Materials: Black and white drawings of common objects.

Procedure: Each student in turn is presented with a set of pictured objects. Say, "Look at the pictures in front of you, and try to remember the order that they are in." Wait a brief interval. "Now, I am going to mix up the pictures and give them back to you. Try to put them back in the same order as they were before I mixed them up."

Start with sequences of three pictures for each child. After each child has succeeded, increase the number of items by one and repeat the procedure.

Note: Almost all visual sequential memory tasks may be made more difficult by increasing the time interval between presentation and recall. Such a delay requires the child to hold the information he has in his memory until he is directed to respond. The trainer may wish to introduce various "rehearsal strategies" to the students, techniques for rehearsing the information and keeping it fresh in memory until the time has come to respond. Rehearsal strategies may include covert auditory rehearsal or the use of visual imagery.

VSM

LESSON 4

Objective: The student will carry out a series of activities first modeled by another student, in the correct sequence.

Materials: None.

Procedure: Say, "I am going to ask one of your classmates to do a series of things. As soon as he (she) has finished, I will ask you to do the very same things in the same order as you saw them done by your classmate. Watch carefully, so that you will be able to do the things you saw your classmate do."

Begin by whispering a series of three directions to a student (e.g., write name on chalkboard, open door, sit in chair). Then ask another student to imitate the sequence without providing any verbal directions. Repeat this procedure, allowing each child a turn to model and imitate. After each child has succeeded with three directions, increase difficulty by adding another direction.

Sample Directions:
1. Write name on chalkboard.
2. Open door, close door.
3. Sit on chair.
4. Hop or skip, forward or backward.
5. Open, book, close book.
6. Draw a circle, square, triangle on paper.
7. Touch toes, head, knees.
8. Lift chair.
9. Clap, snap fingers.
10. Sharpen pencil.
11. Erase chalkboard.

VSM

LESSON 5

Objective: The student will duplicate a bead-stringing sequence which is first modeled by the trainer.

Materials: Box of different colored and shaped beads and bead string.

Procedure: Say, "I am going to string some beads in a certain order. I want you to watch carefully so you can remember the exact order of the beads which I string. When I am finished, I will ask you to string the beads in the exact same order as the ones I strung."

After trainer has strung bead sequence, remove the beads from the string and ask the student to duplicate the sequence from memory, without any additional verbal instructions.

Start with a sequence of three colored beads, all of the same shape, for each child. After each child has succeeded, increase the sequence by one bead and repeat procedure.

The task can be made more difficult by introducing various combinations of colors and shapes into the sequence, or by adding different multiples of each bead to be strung.

VSM

LESSON 6

Objective: The student will remember a designated sequence of visual symbols and step from one to the next in the correct order.

Materials: Two sets of eight visual symbol cards:

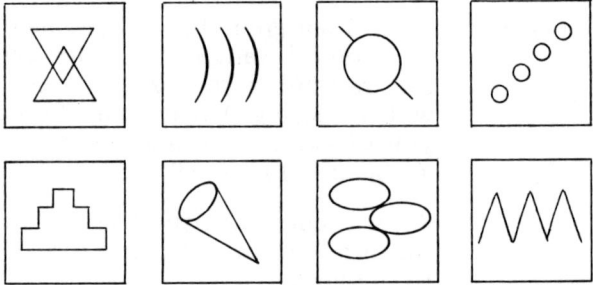

Procedure: Arrange one set of eight visual symbol cards on the floor in a random fashion. Say, "I am going to show you some cards that I want you to step on. After I show them to you close your eyes and try to remember the cards. Then open your eyes, and try to step on the cards in the same order as I showed them to you."

Start with sequences of two visual symbols for each student. After each student has succeeded, increase the number of items by one and repeat the procedure.

Note: This activity involves memory for sequences of visual symbols that are not easily labelled verbally. Since verbal mediation is very difficult in this activity, it provides a good measure of the student's capacity for remembering visual sequences without the aid of verbal cues.

VSM

LESSON 7

Objective: The student will remember a sequence of land-marks, and will rearrange them into the correct order after shuffling.

Materials: Set of landmark cards.

Procedure: Each student in turn is presented with three cards, each depicting an object that serves as a landmark. Say, "I want you to make believe that on the way to school, you have to pass each of the things pictured on your cards. Look at the pictures carefully and try to remember the order that they are in." Wait a brief interval. "Now, I am going to mix up the pictures and give them back to you. I want you to put them back into the same order as they were before, the order that you would pass them on the way to school."

After the student has rearranged the cards, mix them up again and say: "Now, I want you to put the pictures in the order that you would pass them if you were going from school to home." This will require the child to reverse the sequence.

Begin with a series of three landmarks for each child. After each child has succeeded, increase the number of landmarks by one and repeat the procedure.

VSM

LESSON 8

Objective: The student will reproduce a visual pattern on a worksheet which is first demonstrated by trainer.

Materials: Worksheet with nine-dot boxes.

Procedure: The students use a worksheet on which nine dots are printed. Say, "I am going to draw some designs by connecting dots, like those you have on your worksheets, in a special way. Watch carefully while I do it on the chalkboard. When I am finished, I will erase the design. Then I want you to make one just like it on your worksheet. Be sure to draw your design exactly the way I draw mine on the board."

Begin by drawing a simple design on a nine-dot box on the chalkboard, and allow the students several seconds to look at it. Then erase the board and ask the students to reproduce it. Check their work and correct any errors. Repeat the procedure with increasingly difficult designs. Examples are given below:

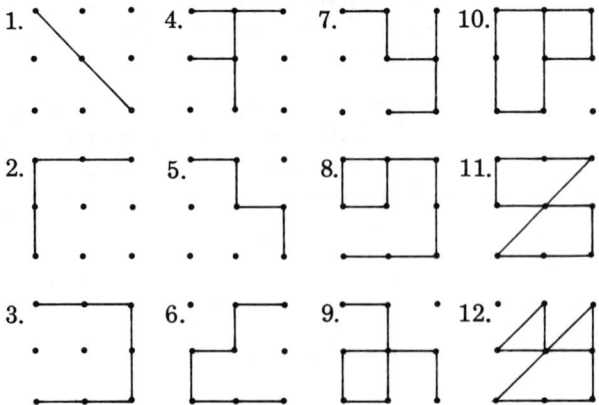

VSM

LESSON 9

Objective: The student will duplicate a sequence of manual gestures without the aid of auditory cues.

Materials: None.

Procedure: Say, "I am going to move my hands in a special way. I want you to watch carefully and when I am finished I will ask one of you (or all of you) to move your hands in the same way that I did."

Begin with a sequence of three manual gestures, holding each position for about three seconds (e.g., hands on head, silent clap, hands on shoulders). After each student has succeeded at this task, increase the sequence of gestures by one and repeat procedure.

Variations in this task may be produced by either prolonging or shortening the time during which each gesture is presented.

Sample Gestures:
1. Hands on head.
2. Hands on shoulders.
3. Arms folded.
4. Silent clap.
5. Right (or left) arm raised.
6. Both arms raised.
7. Arms held forward (or to the sides).
8. Hands on cheeks.
9. Fists on chest.
10. Hands on waist, knees, toes.

VSM

LESSON 10

Objective: The student will remember a designated sequence of positions and step from one position to the next in the correct sequence.

Materials: None.

Procedure: Draw a square divided into four quadrants on the chalkboard and reproduce the pattern on the floor with chalk, string, tape, or any other material. Say, "I am going to tap out a series of movements on the boxes on the board. After I finish, I want you to step from box to box on the floor in the same order as I tapped them out on the board. Watch carefully so you will be able to remember the exact way I go from box to box."

Begin with two movements, starting in one box and moving to two different boxes. Have each student stand in the corresponding starting box on the floor and step from one box to the next duplicating the pattern tapped on the board. Be sure that the students understand the orientation of the floor boxes with respect to those displayed on the board.

As the students progress in this exercise, it may be made more challenging by using a six- and then an eight-box design.

Note: Holding each gesture for a longer period of time will increase the delay between the onset of the trainer's sequence and the reproduction of the sequence by the students. For some students, the delay might facilitate recall in that it would provide additional time for coding and rehearsing the sequence. For other students, the mere fact that a delay has been imposed and the sequence must be held in memory for a longer period of time will negatively affect recall.

Input: Visual or Tactile
Output: Motor or Verbal

VSM

LESSON 11

Objective: The student will repeat from memory a sequence of letters presented visually or "written" on his back.

Materials: Letter Cards.

Procedure: Have the students seated in pairs. Ask one student to come up to you. Say, "I want your partner to put his head down on his desk. I am going to show all the others some letters. Try to remember them in order, so that you can "write" the letters, with the eraser end of your pencil, on the back of your partner. Your partner will wait until you are through writing all your letters and then he will say them out loud in the same order in which you wrote them."

Repeat the procedure for every one of the student pairs. Remember to change the role of the partners in each pair.

Input: Visual/Tactile
Output: Visual/Motor

VSM

LESSON 12

Objective: The student will retrieve hidden geometric shapes, by touch, according to a previously presented visual sequence.

Materials: Set of geometric shapes in a bag.

Procedure: Show the students the bag with the different geometric shapes and identify each of the shapes by name. Put them back into the bag and say, "I am going to place on a table a sequence of shapes. Look at the sequence carefully, because I will cover it up and then ask you to reach into the bag, take out the same shapes, and arrange them in the same order as you saw them. After you have finished, we can take the cover off my sequence and see if it matches yours."

Begin with sequences of three shapes and increase the length of the sequences gradually. The task may be made more difficult by shortening the amount of time allowed for viewing the sample sequence, or by increasing the interval between presentation and recall.

Input: Visual
Output: Visual/Motor

VSM

LESSON 13

Objective: The student will remember a list of objects previously presented to him visually and will recognize and rearrange them in the presented sequence.

Materials: Set of picture cards. This set includes cards with drawings of objects (i.e., food items, utensils) that can be useful on a picnic or a camping trip.

Procedure: Say, "Let us pretend that we are going on a class picnic, and you are asked to bring along the things that are in the pictures I am placing on your desk." Place three picture cards in front of the student. Say, "Now look at the cards and try to remember the things that are drawn on them and the order in which they are arranged." Remove the cards from the student's desk and mix them with ten other cards. Then place all 13 cards in front of the student and say, "Now I want you to look at these cards and choose the things that you were supposed to bring. Can you remember them? Take them out and put them aside on your desk."

If the student succeeds in this task, ask him to rearrange the cards that he chose in the order they were originally presented to him.

Note: This is a difficult task of sequential memory. The difficulty in the task stems from the number of intervening activities between the presentation of the sequence and the student's reproduction of it. If a student has difficulty carrying out this task successfully, modify the task by reducing the number of intervening activities. For example, present the cards, let the student look at them, then mix them up and ask the student to rearrange the cards in the original sequence.

In general, the number of intervening activities between presentation of items to be remembered and their recall represents one aspect affecting the difficulty level of a memory task.

Input: Visual
Output: Visual/Motor

VSM

LESSON 14

Objective: The student will remember a sequence of "words" in sign language.

Materials: Code for signing words in sign language.

Procedure: Say, "I am sure that you all know that some people cannot hear and speak the way we do. They talk to each other by sign language; they make the words with their hands and 'listen' with their eyes. For example, if they want to ask for a hot dog and tea, they make these signs:

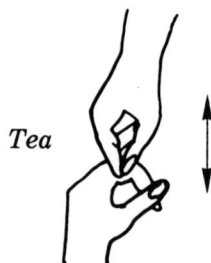

Hot Dog

Tea

Now, I am going to tell you something in sign language and I want you to remember every sign I make so that you can 'tell' it to all the other students in the group."

Start with a sequence of three signs and add new signs gradually. Try to encourage the students to carry out meaningful conversations in sign language.

Note: A beginner's dictionary of sign language may be found in Josef I. Sanders (Ed.) *The ABC's of sign language.* Manca Press, Inc.: Tulsa, Oklahoma, 1968.

Input: Visual
Output: Visual/Motor

VSM

LESSON 15

Objective: The student will remember the order of a series of letter combinations, presented visually, and combine them in writing.

Materials: Sound Blending Cards.

Procedure: Say, "I am going to show you a few cards, one after the other. Look at each card carefully and try to remember the letter combination that is written on each card. After I finish showing you the cards, I want you to write down the letter combinations you saw in the same order as they were presented. If you do this correctly you will end up with a word." Let each child in turn have a chance to write the word on the board and identify it for the others.

Start with two-letter combination cards and proceed by adding cards to form longer and thus more difficult words.

Input: Visual
Output: Visual/Motor

VSM

LESSON 16

Objective: The student will recall a series of visually presented food items following intervening activities.

Materials: Three sets of food item cards.

Procedure: Say, "We are going to play a make-believe game. Let's make believe that we are in a big new school cafeteria where you can order anything you would like to eat. Some of us have to work at this cafeteria too. There is one thing you have to be very careful about: there is no talking in this special cafeteria, and if you want to order something, you have to show the waiter the picture of the food you want. Some of you will be the customers who come to eat at the cafeteria; others will be the cooks and waiters."

Break the students up into groups of three. Assign to one of them the role of a "customer," to a second the role of the "waiter," and to the third the role of the "cook." Give every one of the three students in a team a set of the food item cards. Ask the customer to select four pictures of food items and place them on his desk in sequence so that the waiter can see them. After the waiter has looked at the customer's cards, he must walk over to the cook and pick out from his set of cards those cards that were "ordered" and display them in the correct sequence for the cook. After these cards are removed, the cook must repeat the same procedure (i.e., selecting and displaying the cards for the waiter to see again). The waiter then walks back to the customer and picks the ordered sequence out from his cards and holds the cards in his hand concealed from the customer. The customer is then asked to repeat his order and the waiter and customer compare their cards to see if they have the same food items in the correct sequence.

In order to increase the complexity of this task, have the customer increase the number of food items which he orders. Rotate the roles played by each student so that each gets a chance to act out every role.

VSM

LESSON 17

Objective: The student will match animal cards with the students who previously chose them.

Materials: Animal cards.

Procedure: Say, "We all wonder at times what it would feel like if we were not ourselves but another kind of animal. If you had your choice, what kind of animal would you like to be?" Give the students a chance to look at the animal cards. When every student has picked his animal, ask everyone in turn to show his animal card to the others. Then, collect the cards and ask one of the students to distribute the animals in the correct order to the children who chose them.

Let each student have a chance to match the animal cards with the students who chose them.

VSM

LESSON 18

Objective: The student will recall, in the correct sequence, a series of letters presented visually. The student will construct several different words from a set of four letters.

Materials: Eight sets of four-letter cards.

Procedure: This "ANAGRAMS" exercise uses letter cards to show all the possible rearrangements of the same four letters to form new words. Start with one child; show him four letters, one at a time, in a word sequence. Have him repeat the letters from memory. Next, lay out the letters to form the word; let him check the letter sequence he remembered against the visible word. Finally, let him (with the group) read the word. Repeat the entire procedure, with a different arrangement of the same letters, with the next child. Keep emphasizing the importance of sequence in forming words.

After going around the group several times, each child may be given a four-letter set and asked to write down (or tell to the group) all of the words which can be arranged from his letters. Words which may be formed from the letter sets are:

1. *stop, tops, pots, spot*
2. *spin, pins, nips, snip*
3. *star, tars, rats, arts*
4. *evil, live, vile, veil*
5. *span, pans, naps, snap*
6. *laps, pals, alps, slap*
7. *stan, tans, ants*
8. *stab, tabs, bats*

VSM

LESSON 19

Objective: The student will repeat, both forward and backward, a series of dance steps first performed by the trainer.

Materials: None.

Procedure: Say, "I am going to show you a series of dance steps. I want you to watch me very carefully and try to remember what steps I am doing, and in what order I am doing them. After I finish, I want all of you to try to do the same steps that I did and in the same order."

Start by demonstrating three dance steps. At the beginning, pause briefly between steps in order to set off the steps as separate units to be remembered. After the students have repeated the sequence successfully, say, "Now, I want all of you to try and do the same steps that I do, but this time in the reverse order, starting with the last step in the sequence and ending with the first." Demonstrate this procedure to the students. For examples of steps which may be used, see ASM, Lesson 19.

Lessons
in
Attention

Table 3

Table 3

Summary Table of the Sensory Channels of Input and Output for All Attention Lesson Plans

Lesson Number	Input				Output			
	Auditory	Visual	Motor	Tactile	Auditory or Verbal	Visual	Motor	Tactile
1	x						x	
2	x				x		x	
3	x	x			x	x		
4	x						x	
5	x				x		x	
6	x	x					x	
7	x					x	x	
8	x					x	x	

9		x				x	x
10	x					x	x
11	x						x
12		x				x	
13	x				x		
14	x				x		
15		x				x	x
16	x	x			x		
17	x						x
18	x					x	x
19		x					x
20	x	x					x

INTRODUCTORY LESSON

THE MEANING OF ATTENTION

Objective: The student will be able to explain what is meant by "attention" and give examples.

Materials: None.

Procedure: Say, "Today we are going to learn what is meant by paying attention. We are paying attention to something when we listen carefully to it, or look carefully at it, or think hard about it, and not to the other things around us.

"Paying attention is sometimes very hard to do. There may be things that we'd like to listen to, look at, or think about, more than the thing we are paying attention to; this would mean that we'd have to try very hard to pay attention to only the one thing we want to pay attention to, and not to any other thing around us.

"Paying attention is a very important part of doing many things. We have to pay attention when we do schoolwork, like reading or writing; but we also must pay attention if we want to hit a ball, or jump rope, or play a game like 'Simon Says.' To do each of these things, you must think very hard about what you are trying to do and not let yourself think about other things that are not important. When we ride bicycles we must pay attention to the traffic signs and the cars in the street so that we don't get hurt. Paying attention sometimes means being careful.

"What are some things that you do every day that you have to pay attention to? What must you pay attention to when you do these things?

What can happen if you don't pay attention?"

Encourage a discussion of activities requiring attention—school, home, play activities; try to emphasize the importance of paying attention to the successful completion of these activities.

ATTENTION (ATT)

LESSON 1

Objective: The student will attend to a spoken sentence and step forward or backward on the basis of a predesignated criterion.

Materials: None.

Procedure: Say, "I am going to read a sentence to you. Listen carefully. If I say the name of an animal in your sentence, step forward as soon as you hear me say it. If there is no animal in your sentence, step backward. If there is more than one animal in your sentence, step forward each time."

Repeat procedure with each student individually. After all students have successfully completed their first sentences, repeat the procedure with sentences based on different criterion (colors, children's names, cities, foods, etc.). Stepping forward or backward may be made contingent upon various aspects of the cue words (i.e., forward for solid food, backward for liquid food) rather than on the presence or absence of cue words.

ATT

LESSON 2

Objective: The students will indicate whether a certain tone is identical to one of two tones previously presented.

Materials: Melody Bells.

Procedure: Place the Melody Bells behind any available object that could serve as a screen. Say, "I am going to ring two bells; listen carefully to their sounds. I will then ring one bell only and you will tell me if this bell was one of the bells that I rang before." Allow every one of the students to have his turn. Then repeat this activity using different bell sounds each time with the following background distractions produced by all the students in the group:

1. Ask the students to hum a tune.
2. Ask the students to sing a song.
3. Ask the students to read a paragraph.

Note: This session requires auditory discrimination skills and the ability to attend to auditory stimuli in the presence of distractors. Thus, it may serve as an indicator of possible deficits in this area of functioning.

ATT

LESSON 3

Objective: The student will attend to a list of object names and select only the predesignated items.

Materials: Black and white drawings of common objects.

Procedure: Each student in turn is presented with three pictured objects. Say, "I am going to say a list of objects very fast. Listen carefully to see if I say any of the things in your pictures. When I am finished, you tell me which of the things in your pictures I said."

Begin with three pictures and a list of ten objects. After each child has succeeded, increase the number of pictures by one and repeat procedure. Be sure not to mention *all* of the pictured objects in the verbally presented list, so the student will have to choose only those pictures which are mentioned.

ATT

LESSON 4

Objective: The student will listen to verbal directions and follow *only* specific directions predesignated by a certain cue.

Materials: None.

Procedure: This may be done as a group activity. Say, "I am going to tell you some things to do. Listen carefully, because I only want you to follow the directions if you hear me say the words 'I say' first. Those of you who know the game 'Simon Says' will find this game very similar. Remember, only do what I tell you to do if you hear me say the words 'I say' first."

This activity may be conducted as an elimination type game, with the winner given the chance to conduct the activity next. For increased interest or difficulty, the cue words may be changed from time to time.

ATT

LESSON 5

Objective: The student will attend to a specific bead-stringing task while disregarding the verbal repetition of bead-stringing instructions by another child.

Materials: Box of differently colored and shaped beads and bead string.

Procedure: This activity is done in pairs, one pair at a time. Place a box of beads (different colors and shapes) between two students. Say, "I want each of you to put on your own string a different combination of two beads. Work at the same time." (Assign two colors to one student and two different colors to the other student.) Say, "As you string your beads, say out loud the kind of bead you are stringing." (Demonstrate procedure.) "Remember to pay attention to only the beads you're supposed to string, no matter what your partner is saying." Start by assigning to each student two colors to string.

The task can be made more challenging by having the students exchange their patterns on a given signal.

ATT

LESSON 6

Objective: The student will attend to verbal directions and follow only those directions predesignated by a certain visual cue.

Materials: Set of eight visual symbol cards.

Procedure: This may be done as a group activity. Hold a different visual symbol card in each hand. Say, "I am going to tell you some things to do, and at the same time I will show you one of these two cards (show the students the cards held in both hands). If I hold up this card (show card in one hand), you should follow my direction and do the thing I said to do. But, if I hold up the other card (show card in other hand), you should not follow my direction, and you shouldn't do the thing I said to do. This game is like the 'Simon Says' game, only we use these picture cards instead of the words 'Simon Says.' Remember, you must watch and listen very carefully, and only do what I tell you to do when I hold up this card (show appropriate card again)."

This activity may be conducted as an elimination type game, with the winner given the chance to conduct the activity next. For increased interest and difficulty, change the cards from time to time.

ATT

LESSON 7

Objective: The student will attend to auditory cues to determine whether to move forward or backward on a picture strip, or withhold movement.

Materials: Picture strip depicting landmarks.

Procedure: Say, "I am going to ask you to start at the picture of the house; make believe this is your home and you are to move forward towards school, which is at the other end of the picture strip. You may proceed from picture to picture only if the traffic light is 'green.' When I tap my pencil once, it means 'green light' and you may move on to the next picture. When I tap my pencil twice, it means 'red light' and you have to stay where you are. I will also tell whether to go forward or go back. You are to do so following the same traffic light sings," (i.e., one pencil tap = green, two taps = red).

Trainer should be sure to follow the correct position for each child as he or she moves along the picture strip, and correct errors immediately.

This task may be made more complex by changing the auditory cues upon which movement is contingent, i.e., one pencil tap + number = go forward, pencil tap + letter = go backward.

ATT

LESSON 8

Objective: The student will attend and respond to one kind of stimulus only while two kinds are presented.

Materials: Worksheet with random numbers and letters.

Procedure: The students use a worksheet on which numbers and letters are printed in random fashion. Say, "I am going to say some numbers and letters, one after the other. I want each of you to listen only for the letters, and as I say a letter, draw a line connecting it with the next letter I say. Remember, pay attention only to the letters." (Demonstrate procedure before starting.)

The same procedure can be repeated with numbers only.

The task can be made more difficult by limiting the target stimuli to *even* numbers only, *odd* numbers only, etc.

Input: Auditory
Output: Visual/Motor

ATT

LESSON 9

Objective: The student will be able to attend to a group gesturing activity and discover who in the group is leading the gesturing.

Materials: None.

Procedure: Have the students sit in a circle. Choose one student to "Scout" and have the student leave the room. While the student is out of the room, designate one member of the group as "Indian Chief." Say, "The Indian Chief will lead us in hand gesturing. We all must pay attention to the 'Chief' and follow his gestures, no matter how he changes them. Remember to change your gestures as soon as the 'Chief' does, so the 'Scout' will have a hard time guessing who the 'Chief' is." After procedure is demonstrated, call the "Scout" back into the room and explain the game to him. Then proceed to play.

Repeat the procedure, with each new "Indian Chief" becoming the next "Scout."

Input: Auditory
Output: Visual/Motor

ATT

LESSON 10

Objective: The student will move from letters to numbers on the floor by responding to one kind of stimulus only while two kinds are presented.

Materials: Number and letter cards.

Procedure: Arrange the number and letter cards on the floor in random fashion. Say, "I am going to ask each of you to start by standing on either a letter or a number. Next, I will say a series of numbers and letters. If you are standing on a *number*, you may only move to the next *letter* that I say; if you are standing on a *letter*, you may only move to the next *number* that I say. You must listen very carefully, so that each time you will only move in the right way at the right time." Demonstrate the procedure so that the students understand the directions.

Begin with a series of letters and numbers, spoken slowly, with only a few trick clues. Increase the difficulty of this task by saying the letters and numbers more rapidly and by increasing the number of trick clues given to each student.

Input: Visual or Tactile
Output: Motor

ATT

LESSON 11

Objective: The student will identify the "non-letter" patterns among a series of letter patterns "written" on his back.

Materials: None.

Procedure: This activity may be carried out as a competitive game involving one representative of each of two student groups. Say, "I am going to ask each of the two 'representatives' to write with the eraser end of a pencil various letter patterns on each other's back. Some of the patterns that they write will be real letters, but other patterns that they write will not be letters. If you think that a pattern that is not a letter was written on your back, raise your hand. The group whose representatives identify correctly all of the 'non-letter' patterns will be the winning group."

The students on whose backs the patterns will be written should be seated with their backs to the board. Write on the board the letters and "non-letters" to be written each time, so that the entire group can follow along.

The game can be made more difficult by including number patterns in the sequences and requiring different responses to number, letter, and non-letter patterns, or any combination of these categories.

Sample "Non-Letter" Patterns:

△ ▽ □ ⟋\ ⟩ ◇ ⫽ ⋂ ⋌ ⑥

ATT

LESSON 12

Objective: The student will focus continuously on the changing position of a hidden object, and locate its final position.

Materials: Four paper cups, two beads of different shape.

Procedure: Place the four cups in front of a student and say, "Watch carefully, I am going to put this bead under one of the cups, and then move the cups around. You have to pay careful attention to the way I move the cups, so that you will know where the bead is all the time without picking up the cups. When I am through moving the cups, I want you to point to the cup with the bead under it."

Move the cups slowly and only a few times at the start. As the students become more proficient, move the cups more rapidly and try to challenge the student's ability to pay continuous attention. To increase complexity, a second bead may be introduced into the game under another cup.

Input: Auditory
Output: Verbal

ATT

LESSON 13

Objective: The student will detect an item missing on the second presentation of a list of "things for a picnic."

Materials: None.

Procedure: Say, "Let us pretend that we are going out on a picnic and we are asked to make up a list of things to bring. I'm going to read a list of picnic items to you. I'll read it twice. The second time I read the list, I will leave out one thing. I want you to pay attention so that you can find the one thing that I left out on our picnic list."

Examples of Item Lists:
1. Hot dogs, soda, chips, tomatoes, apples.
2. Sleeping bags, blankets, crackers, chocolates.
3. Nuts, candy, bananas, first-aid kit.
4. Apples, bread, bananas, crackers, chocolates, soda.

(Any part of these lists or combinations of them may be used.)

ATT

LESSON 14

Objective: The student will attend to a sentence and identify his target words.

Materials: None.

Procedure: Say, "We are going to play a game. I will tell each of you to pay attention to one category of words, like color words, food words, children's names, days of the week, or numbers. (Assign a word category to each of the students.) Now, I will say some sentences to you. Every time I say a sentence, I want each of you to try and figure out whether the sentence I said included a word from your category. If the sentence *did* include your kind of word, raise your hand and tell me what that word was."

Alternate the sentences so that every student's category is included frequently.

Sample Sentences:
1. The children ran to the beach to fly their blue kite.
2. Elephants love to eat peanuts.
3. Danny had a birthday party last Saturday.
4. We have one little puppy and three gold fish.

Note: This task requires not only attention to the sentence and recognition of the target word, but also the ability to categorize and generalize. The student must be able to recognize the relationship between the word category assigned to him and one representative of this category in the sentence read to him. In order to make this task simpler for some students, assign to them categories that are more concrete (i.e., colors or animals) than abstract (i.e., feelings or activities).

ATT

LESSON 15

Objective: The student will detect and respond to a visually presented letter combination embedded in different words presented visually.

Materials: Word cards and Sound Blending Cards.

Procedure: Say, "First I am going to show you a card with a few letters on it. Then, I am going to show you some cards with words on them. I want you to look at the word cards and tell me whether any of these words contain the combination of letters that you saw on the first card. Each time you see a word that has those letters in it, clap your hands."

This task can be made more challenging by requiring students to shift their response (i.e., lifting an arm instead of clapping hands) according to the trainer's instructions.

ATT

LESSON 16

Objective: The student will listen to a verbally presented list of food items while simultaneously attending to visually presented cues; he will alter his verbal response to the food items in line with the visual cues.

Materials: Letter cards.

Procedure: Organize the students into pairs and work with one pair at a time. Say, "Today we will pretend we have a restaurant. One of you will be the waiter and someone else will give the order. I will stand in back of the customer, facing the waiter, and will show the waiter a card with a letter on it. The waiter will have to tell the customer that he is out of all the foods which start with the letter that I am showing. As soon as the customer orders something that the waiter is out of, he must say, 'We don't have any today.'" (Demonstrate procedure.)

The task can be made more difficult by having the restaurant "out" of all foods starting with either of two letters.

ATT

LESSON 17

Objective: The student will attend to a list of commands and respond selectively to predesignated name cues.

Materials: None.

Procedure: Say, "We all wonder at times what it would feel like if we had been given a different first name. Each of you now has a chance to choose any first name he would like other than his own and tell it to the group. Then, I am going to ask you to do different things (i.e., lift hand, touch toes, stamp feet). You are supposed to do what I say only if I mention your *new* name. Remember, respond to your new name only!"

Let each child have a turn at giving directions as well as following them.

ATT

LESSON 18

Objective: The students will attend to number sequences and respond selectively to numbers containing target sounds.

Materials: None.

Procedure: Invite one student at a time to the board and say, "This student is going to write all the numbers on the board that you will tell him to write. Each of you will have a turn telling numbers. Before we start, we have to decide on two letters, any two letters you choose, which will be our target letters. Every time one of you suggests to the student at the board a number that contains one of the target letters, the student at the board has to write that number down and draw a circle around it. Say your numbers quickly so that the student writing them will have to pay careful attention in order to notice which ones contain the target letters.

The target letters may be changed from time to time in order to require the exercise of selective attention.

ATT

LESSON 19

Objective: The student will selectively carry out dance steps according to a predesignated visual cue provided by the trainer.

Materials: None.

Procedure: This activity is done in pairs, one pair at a time. Have two students stand in front of the group, facing the trainer, and say, "Watch and listen carefully. I am going to do some dance steps. Sometimes I will place my hands on my waist as I do the steps and other times I will not. I want one of you to imitate only those steps that I do with my hands on my waist; the other will imitate only those steps I do without my hands on my waist. You have to watch carefully and pay attention so you will be able to follow only those steps that you are supposed to."

Demonstrate the procedure before beginning. The speed at which the steps are performed may be increased to add difficulty. Complexity may be introduced by varying the cue upon which the student's discriminations are based, or by having the students exchange the cue they had been responding to on a given signal.

LIST OF MATERIALS

Lesson	ASM	VSM	ATT
1	—	Visual Symbol Cards	—
2	Melody Bells	Melody Bells	Melody Bells
3	Cards of Common Objects	Cards of Common Objects	Cards of Common Objects
4	—	—	—
5	Box of Colored Beads and String	Box of Colored Beads and String	Box of Colored Beads and String
6	Color Cards	Visual Symbol Cards	Visual Symbol Cards
7	Landmark Cards	Landmark Cards	Landmark Cards
8	Letter and Number Worksheet	Letter and Number Worksheet	Letter and Number Worksheet
9	—	—	—

#	Column 1	Column 2	Column 3
10	Number and Letter Cards	—	Number and Letter Cards
11	—	Letter Cards	—
12	Geometric Shapes in Bag	Geometric Shapes in Bag	Cups and Beads
13	—	Picnic Item Cards	—
14	—	Sign Language Cards	—
15	—	Sound Blending Cards	Word Cards and Sound Blending Cards
16	—	Food Item Cards	Letter Cards
17	—	Animal Cards	—
18	—	Letter Cards	—
19	—	—	—
20	Folding Paper	Folding Paper	Folding Paper